SHENZHEN SUPERSTARS

How China's smartest city
is challenging Silicon Valley

Johan Nylander

shenzhensuperstars.com

MY FREE GIFT TO YOU

If you would like a unique list of co-working offices, accelerators, maker spaces and technology parks in Shenzhen, please e-mail me at shenzhensuperstars@gmail.com with subject FREE GIFT.

This is my way of saying thanks for purchasing this book.

INTRODUCTION

This one-hour-read is about the fastest growing city in history – Shenzhen.

It's the story about how a Chinese fishing village became a global economic powerhouse of innovation and technology. Just four decades ago Shenzhen was a backwater area, populated by subsistence fishermen and rice farmers. Today, it's home to up to 20 million people and some of the world's leading technology companies and most innovative tech startups.

No other city better symbolizes the rise of modern China. And no other city challenges Silicon Valley more aggressively as the global hub for innovation and technology startups. In many ways, the Chinese city has already outsmarted the Valley.

This e-book is written for anyone who wants to be part of this raging growth story – no matter if you're a tech buff, investor or just someone curious about knowing what's driving the future.

As a journalist for CNN, Forbes and other international media, I has witnessed the astonishing transformation of the south Chinese city. Its speed, energy and determination are just mind-blowing. My aim is to take you inside, to the very heart of what is shaping this vibrant city.

The e-book of Shenzhen Superstars became the bestseller on Amazon's China section.

Happy reading.

KEY QUOTES FROM THE BOOK

"In terms of hardware plus software innovation,
Shenzhen is ahead of the curve."
– Jeffrey Towson, private equity investor and
Peking University professor

"The next ten years will be the era of robots and intelligent
machines, and Shenzhen will play well to that."
– Jixun Foo, managing partner of GGV Capital

"Shenzhen is just better than Silicon Valley in terms of
hardware and software integration."
– Qin Li, CEO of startup Sennotech

"If you're not already in Shenzhen, you're crazy."
– Edith Yeung, general partner of 500 Startups

ABOUT THE AUTHOR

Johan Nylander is an award-winning author and freelance China and Asia correspondent. He is frequently published by CNN, Forbes and Sweden's leading business daily Dagens Industri.

For almost two decades, Nylander has covered news from a wide range of countries.

Today, he spends most of his time traveling around China and neighboring countries, conducting interviews with the people who will shape the Asia of tomorrow: presidents and peasants, entrepreneurs and migrant workers, triad members and government officials.

During the 2008 financial crisis he was stationed as a foreign correspondent in London. He has an MBA from the University of Gothenburg in his native Sweden, and is the author of an acclaimed management book called Simplify (Förenkla!, Liber publishing).

Nylander lives with his family in Hong Kong.

For more about him and updates on upcoming e-books, visit johannylander.asia or amazon.com/author/johannylander.

TABLE OF CONTENTS

WHEN THE IPHONE HACKER CAME TO TOWN

When Silicon Valley veteran Scotty Allen first came to the southern Chinese city of Shenzhen a few years ago as part of an organized tour for American tech geeks, and witnessed the city's noisy hardware and electronics markets, its buzzing tech startup scene and countless glittering skyscrapers, his spontaneous reaction was not: "Wow, this is cool." It was: "Wow, we are fucked".

That was in 2015, and it was a visit that turned out to be a life-changing experience. He realized that something unique was happening in this Chinese city – a city that he, along with most of his colleagues and friends in the US, were not aware of. To put it starkly, he knew that China was about to outsmart the West in terms of technology.

"Coming to Shenzhen is like visiting the future. But it's this crazy Blade Runner-esque future", says Allen, his bearded, somewhat wild-looking face beaming in a broad smile. "There's this incredible energy here. There's a sort of feeling that like all boats are rising. People are just really smart and really innovative and really creative."

We meet in a coffee shop in the downtown area. It's Tuesday evening, and outside on the noisy street puddles reflect the light from small noodle bars' neon signage. Well-dressed office workers and young students hasten for the metro station, their faces illuminated by the screens on their mobile phones, to which their eyes are glued. A garbage man is swiping up electronic waste from the sidewalk, and I can see an old woman dismantling an air conditioner for scrap parts. Some buildings are modern and futuristic while others look ready to be torn down. Small hole-in-the-wall shops display everything from mobile phones and mini drones to pets and handbags. The subtropical summer heat is sticky.

Thirty-eight year old Allen is originally from south California and calls himself a software engineer by training and an entrepreneur by personality. He spent several years as a software engineer at Google, specializing in search infrastructure and user experience, then bounced around at a number of prominent startups in the Valley, including Ooyala and Shopkick. Working for these companies was amazing, he says, , adding that he worked with super smart people. But it also involved "working my butt off and getting totally burned out". After starting his own company, Appmonsta – a big-data firm that provides app marketplace information – he realized he was still struggling to find his place and meaning in the corporate environment. "We were writing a whole bunch of code and sold contracts to Fortune 500 companies and did large scale enterprise sales. And I hated it", he tells me. "So I fired myself."

He ended up in Shenzhen via the above-mentioned hacker trip to China, which was organized by a friend he'd met through the Noisebridge hacker space in San Francisco. Some two dozens tech enthusiasts participated in that trip, which also took in Hong Kong, Shanghai and Beijing. In Shenzhen the group visited several open-source hardware companies (including Seeed Studio and Dangerous Prototypes) and hacker spaces (Chaihuo Makerspace and SZDIY), and they were also shown around town by local tech buffs.

What made the most profound impression on Allen was

the city's exhilaratingly buzzy, noisy Huaqiangbei electronics market. The largest hub in the world for electronic components, it offers everything from circuit boards to LED lights, drones and computer-controlled cutting machines – all at remarkably low prices. Tech Radar once called Shenzhen "the global gadget capital", and I'm pretty sure they were referring to the Mecca that is Huaqiangbei. The area is basically a one-mile strip with ten-story buildings on both sides of the boulevard filled to the brim with electrical stuff, both legal and illegal. It's any tech nerd's candy store.

Scotty Allen was sold.

"I came to Shenzhen and totally fell in love with it. When we were done in Beijing I immediately bought a train ticket back here to Shenzhen. And I've coming and going ever since," he says.

He admits, somewhat reluctantly, that like many other Westerners he had a prejudiced – or at least uninformed – view of China as a poor country with an economy based on low-level manufacturing and cheap piracy.

"I'm kind of ashamed to admit this, but I came in with the attitude that China is far behind the US – a place where we farm out the stuff that we don't want to do," he says. "It was an attitude of superiority. But the reality was very different. I realized there was a more money here than I thought there was. It was way higher tech. The infrastructure was way better. In most ways, Shenzhen is actually a nicer city than San Francisco."

Today Allen has become a specialist on the south Chinese city's electronics-manufacturing scene – the industrial markets, factories and back alleys where the world's electronics are made. You might actually already have heard about him. Allen is that guy who built his own iPhone from the ground up by using only recycled and spare parts that he found at the local electronics markets.

The inspiration to do so came one boozy evening at a barbecue joint in the city when a friend speculated whether it might be possible. Scotty took up the challenge. Initially, he wasn't even sure whether he would able to source all the parts. On his popular Youtube channel Strange Parts he documents scouting around dozens of small stores at the electronic markets in search of the components needed for his phone's screen, shell, battery and logic board. The video takes you from the main markets to hidden alleys, even to a cellphone repair school. The process was far from easy, and on several occasions he had to return to the same store to replace components or seek advice. But eventually, with many a teachable moment along the way, he was able to build a completely functional iPhone 6s. Allen says the phone's parts cost him about US$300. By comparison, an iPhone 6S from Apple starts at around $550.

Sitting at the café, he shows me the phone and I play around with it for a while. I can't honestly tell it's not an original. I'm far from an expert but I've tried out many iPhone and Android rip-offs in China and you can normally tell a fake one instantly. Scotty's, though, is just perfect: the screen swipes easily; apps open and close; the camera and compass work, as do all the other apps I try out. Scotty emphasizes that it's not a rip-off – it's a remake of mainly recycled parts, just like building a car from old parts from the scrap yard. The project whetted his appetite and on his Youtube channel you can watch even geekier DIY adventures from the streets of Shenzhen.

Making the iPhone was more than a fun hobby project. It was an experiment to see whether Shenzhen could deliver on its reputation as a gadget utopia. The city passed the test, and Allen does not think it would be possible to make a phone from scratch like this in any other part of the world.

"The availability in Shenzhen is phenomenal. I can walk to the markets 10 or 15 minutes from where I'm staying and find a lot of the parts I need. Anything rare that I can't find myself can be delivered to me within a day. In the States, for hobbyist level stuff it takes closer to weeks and it is many times the price.

"This is unique. I think this is one of the first places where it really feels like just about anything is possible."

Part of the equation is that Shenzhen is more than just a city. It's the heart of the Pearl River Delta, one of China's most powerful business and manufacturing clusters, and is situated right by the border to Hong Kong, one of the world's leading financial centers and still an important gateway between East and West. While the dirtiest factories have now left Shenzhen itself and the city is increasingly built on high finance, high tech and creativity, it remains surrounded by the world's most complete supply chain for hardware manufacturing.

This infrastructure has created one of the world's most powerful hubs for manufacturing smart hardware. While the US is dominant in the software field, China – and especially Shenzhen and the Pearl River Delta – has the advantage in hardware.

Numerous American and Asian entrepreneurs interviewed for this book, not to mention international venture capitalists, are clear that Shenzhen is streets ahead in a lot of areas, from robotics to self-driving cars.

For Scotty, who has spent years getting to know what makes the US' and China's main innovation hubs unique, this is strikingly obvious.

"Silicon Valley in San Francisco is no longer Silicon Valley. It's really Software Valley. I don't think there's much good hardware innovation in the Valley. Shenzhen is definitely the new Silicon Valley in terms of hardware production", he says.

Today, companies in Shenzhen already spend more on research and development than in any other city in China, and innovation-driven sectors – from ICT to biotech – make up bigger parts of its economy than anywhere else. In fact, companies in Shenzhen apply for more international patents than the whole of the United Kingdom. (We'll dive deeper into numbers later in the book.)

The city is home to some of the world's leading and most innovative technology companies, many of them firms that people in the West probably haven't heard of. Let's just look at some of the headline acts. Shenzhen has one of the world's biggest internet companies (Tencent recently surpassed Facebook in market value), the world's biggest maker of drones (Anyone flying past DJI lately? Not likely), the world's biggest maker of plug-in electric cars (Nope, it's not Tesla, it's BYD); and the world's biggest telecoms equipment company (Huawei is three times bigger than its closest rival, Sweden's Ericsson).

Oh, and did I mention where Apple has set up its latest research and development center? No prizes for guessing. The city is also home to some of the most inspirational startup entrepreneurs I've ever met, with businesses ranging from financial, medical and education technology to wealth management and hospitality. On one occasion I got a ride in a taxi that the cabbie had turned into mobile version of a 7-Eleven, selling everything from nuts and dried mango to umbrellas via QR codes and mobile payments. Many of the city's tech startups (okay, maybe not the taxi guy) already have valuations of millions of dollars, and are breaking new ground in everything from financial services, automation and robotics to artificial intelligence and virtual reality.

While there are many factors connecting Silicon Valley and Shenzhen – people are, stereotypically, young, hungry and highly educated – Scotty also sees striking differences in behavior. In the US, if you have an idea, the assumption is that you're going to use what you have available to make everything yourself. In China, people are more likely to work in a network of other people, he explains. It's all about whom you know and who has the right machines to help you with your prototype. Vertical integration, where one company can do the entire project soup to nuts, is less common here. Allen's biggest tip for people coming to Shenzhen is to be prepared to jump in with both feet and be ready to engage with the community. This is not a situation where you can show up with a design, throw it over the wall, and expect to get back a perfect production run or a perfect prototype, he says.

"Expect to go to factories to get your hands dirty. Talk with the engineers and the workers. Also, expect that things will go wrong. Manufacturing is hard. But if you approach it from the perspective of a partnership, that you're working together as a team with the factory, you can get really high results. You're going to need to put in the hours."

Even if many products are still getting designed in San Francisco, they are, for the most part, being manufactured here in Shenzhen, he says. Or, if they're not, they're still using parts coming out of Shenzhen. In hardware, at least if you need volume, it's just hard not to touch upon Shenzhen.

For Scotty Allen, however, what's important is not whether Shenzhen or Silicon Valley is ahead. It's more about both doing great, and existing in symbiosis, rather than as rivals. He no longer sees it as the US versus China, but rather a situation where all advance together, he explains. He does, however, encourage more Westerners to come to Shenzhen and experience the amazing development and opportunities in the city.

As he sips his tea, I ask Allen to explain the one thing that for him defines the city, that special detail that makes it what it is. Again, his bearded face shines up in a broad smile.

"Shenzhen has an energy of growth – the same energy I felt when I first came to Silicon Valley ten years ago," he says. "And it's not just in technology. It's this idea that whoever you are, whatever you're into, you can come to China, and especially Shenzhen, and do it!"

WORLD'S FASTEST GROWING CITY

If Scotty Allen had stood in the same place and said the things he told me for this book 40 years ago, people would probably have laughed and written him off as the local fool.

The transformation Shenzhen has undergone is unique – truly unique – in history. Our remarkable story starts in a backwater area, populated by subsistence fishermen and rice farmers, on the border of Hong Kong, then still a British colony, by the Pearl River Delta in south China. Its population was poor and uneducated.

It's a slight exaggeration to say that Shenzhen was a "sleepy fishing village," as media and policy makers love to portray it as. When Deng Xiaoping – the country's de facto leader after Mao Zedong – officially gave Shenzhen city-status in 1979 and the following year designated it China's first Special Economic Zone, only 30,000 people lived there. The wider area that today makes up Shenzhen housed more than 300,000 people, however. That's about half the number of people in Sweden's second-largest industrial town, Gothenburg, where I grew up – and no-one would call Gothenburg a "sleepy fishing village". Shenzhen also had the advantage of being squeezed in between the world's largest port city (Hong Kong) and Guangzhou, the provincial capital of Guangdong, cities which were home to five and two million people, respectively, in 1980. The area was in essence a large, scattered patchwork of paddy fields, orchards and fishing villages, but it also had early private markets and factories.

Professor Ezra F. Vogel, one of the world's most celebrated

China watchers, set foot in Shenzhen – and China – for the first time in 1973. In the foreword to a insightful book called Learning from Shenzhen – edited by Mary Ann O'Donnell, Winnie Wong and Jonathan Bach, and published this year – Vogel explains what Shenzhen looked like then as he walked across the border bridge from Hong Kong:

"In the market town [of Shenzhen] are large numbers of state owned stores, and there is a factory making cement, another making bricks, one making limited kind of machinery which is used to repair various tractors and other machinery. There are also two small fertilizer factories which make various kinds of fertilizer. In addition to the large number of state-owned stores, there is a private market […] where farmers can bring their tiny amount of vegetables they grow on their private plots. Most of the adults in the village were engaged in industry, commerce and service work, serving the surrounding countryside."

Vogel also goes into some detail about Deng's visit to Shenzhen on the eve of unveiling his 1978 Reform and Opening policy. Deng disagreed with other politicians in China who said that the flow of refugees into Hong Kong – many of whom risked their lives to swim across Shenzhen Bay – was a public security issue that should be dealt with by clamping down and policing the border. The basic problem, Deng argued, was economics. The economy on the Chinese side of the border had fallen too far behind and it was understandable that young people should flee to Hong Kong where they were promised opportunities for a better way of life. The answer, he said, was in economic development on the Chinese side of the border.

Deng might also have been inspired by Taiwan and South Korea, both of which had by this time opened widely successfully trade and export processing zones.

The growth that followed after Shenzhen became China's first economic experiment – a place where foreign and domestic trade could take place without the explicit authorization of China's central government – is matchless in history. In the early 1980s, manufacturing enterprises started to emerge in Luohu, Futian and Shekou – areas that make up present-day central Shenzhen. The city quickly became a hotbed of young intellectuals and career-minded officials who wanted a more exciting and freer life, according to Vogel. Already in 1980, young intellectuals who wanted to go to the West but did not have the opportunity to do so flocked to Shenzhen.

During his legendary Southern Tour in 1992, Deng – the chain-smoking, five-foot titan of China's economic reform – famously proclaimed: "Let some people get rich first." Since then, Shenzhen has been flooded with thousands of foreign investors and millions of domestic workers hoping to improve their lot. Tax incentives and freedom to trade without the approval of the Chinese government helped Shenzhen to lure Hong Kong manufacturers and investors to open factories here, giving rise to the epithet that Shenzhen was "the playground of Hong Kong's rich." Part of the city's success, according to a report by the Brookings Institution and JPMorgan, came from the fact that productivity rose and cutting-edge production technologies were embraced much faster in Shenzhen than in other Chinese cities, or indeed in Western economies generations before.

For years, as it industrialised, the common image of Shenzhen wasn't pretty. Through the 1980s and 1990s, Shenzhen was considered to be a cheap and rather soulless manufacturing base. Global news reports of pollution, poor factory conditions and worker suicides exacerbated the city's image as an anonymous and brutal place. To understand what Shenzhen looked like during its early decades of development – and in fact still does in its less developed areas – one only needs to visit neighboring cities in the Pearl River Delta. Shenzhen's closest neighbor, Dongguan, now has a reputation as the "the world's factory": for a time it produced more than a third of the world's toys, as well as mountains of shoes, furniture and other low-quality mass-market products. The city still looks today like one huge factory, and smells like one too. Industrial plants fight for space with warehouses and grey-brown buildings where workers live in dormitories. Wide highways thunder through the city, conveying lorries that cough out dark clouds of exhaust fumes. Most people living there are factory workers.

When I first moved to Hong Kong, in 2011, I only knew Shenzhen and the Pearl River Delta by its tarnished reputation. In fact, many of our new friends in Hong Kong warned us against going there. It was, they said, a shithole. And indeed, my first encounter with the city was less than charming. From our hotel window we could see dozens of rats run up and down the façade of a residential building – and into occupied rooms through broken windows. It must have been delightful for the rats, because we also saw residents throwing garbage from their balconies right onto the street below.

As I started traveling to the city more regularly, however – and began finding my way around the downtown entertainment and shopping areas and the main technology parks – I started to grow a liking for it. Today I go there often, mainly for work but often just to hang out with friends at any of the many craft beer bars or excellent local restaurants. And over the years I have witnessed an almost mind-blowing transformation. Whole neighborhoods have become unrecognizable, skyscrapers shooting up like bamboo grooves and new shopping malls spreading like wildfire. Rusty old trucks have given way to comfy electrical cars and colorful bicycles from the many bike-sharing companies. A city once known for copycat products has emerged as a world-class cluster of innovation. Walking down any of the city's tech parks or finance districts is to be offered a glimpse into a future economy.

"The dirtiest factories have left Shenzhen," says Phoebe Chen, CEO of Harmony Family Office, a startup wealth management company. "Today, the city is built on high finance, high tech and creativity. There is a special atmosphere that you won't find anywhere else. There is a constant energy and a special dynamic here."

We meet at her quite extraordinary office in one of the city's tallest skyscrapers. The entire office is decorated in traditional Chinese style. As a visitor, there is a sense of having entered an ancient teahouse, one with low, chunky wooden furniture and walls covered in calligraphy. It's stunningly beautiful, and one feels instinctively at ease. A water fountain stands in the foyer beside a bamboo vase.

Chen herself is clad in traditional Chinese garments, the picture of elegance.

"When our clients come to us, they should feel that we care about them," she says, as, with practiced hand, she performs the honors in a gongfu tea ceremony, pouring the hot liquid into tiny little cups. "If we are going to help them manage their assets and inheritance from one generation to the next, they have to feel a sense of harmony here. Many of our clients trust neither the government nor big banks, so they have to be able to trust us."

Chen and her three colleagues all made their careers in international banking, working for institutions such as Citibank and Standard Chartered. Their new firm is aimed at China's super rich – people with fortunes of at least 10 million yuan (US$1.5 million). It's their way of generating their own fortune but also, perhaps even more importantly, of working on their own terms. Harmony Family Office is just one of many examples of how Shenzhen has been transformed from a polluted factory town into a modern metropolis with a modern economy, and how creativity and out-of-the-box thinking are becoming key to all kinds of businesses.

At the same interview, or tea ceremony, I speak with Ada Lo, a woman in her 20s who was born in Shenzhen. She used to work with Chen at Citibank. Her role was to advise wealthy clients on how to invest their riches – a prestigious job worth holding onto, one might think. But the Shenzhen spirit got the better of her, too. Today, she's rolling out a chain of hostels.

"Basically, nobody in Shenzhen wants to be employed", she explains.

Over the course of several trips to Shenzhen, I asked residents both young and old what drives the city. What is the key to its success? Everyone gave me the same answer: an unabashed spirit of entrepreneurship.

In fact, no other city in China is home to more people who want to start their own business. According to a survey by the Sweden-based employer-branding company Universum, more than 60 percent of post-1990s university graduates in Shenzhen say they want to join a startup or start their own company. In Beijing, only 15 percent have similar dreams.

It's not just business and the local economy that are in a state of conversion, though. In terms of liveability and lifestyle, the city has undergone enormous changes, adding new parks and restaurant areas, better housing and improved air quality. Cocktail lounges and sport bars have expanded all over the city, from Coco Park to Shekou Seaworld, while fashionable shopping malls seem to be everywhere. When Japanese lifestyle brand Muji thought about setting up its first-ever design hotel, its owners didn't choose Tokyo, New York or any other city famous for its hip urban culture – they chose Shenzhen. Check out Shenzhen Party for events, eateries and happenings around the city.

Jessica Luo, an art gallery worker who grew up in Shenzhen, says there is an entirely different pulse in the city today compared to just a few years ago.

"My friends and I used to always head down to Hong Kong to go clubbing and find new trends and cultures before," she said. "Now we stay here. This is where things are happening."

One example of that change is OCT Loft. This is an old factory area that has been transformed into one of the country's most vibrant cultural and artistic enclaves. Art galleries and book cafes jostle for space with art studios and music clubs on leafy pedestrian walkways. Building fronts still maintain a factory-roughened look but many of the stores and restaurants are meticulously styled.

Here you'll find Mann Li's café, Gee Coffee. With the scent of freshly-ground coffee in the air, local hipsters mingle with tourists and freelancers with their laptops. Mann Li first encountered coffee when he was exporting electronic components to Ethiopia and decided to start shipping beans back to China.

"When the market prices for beans plummeted a few years ago, we were sitting on a huge inventory and lost almost all our money," he says as we sip espressos, perhaps the best I have ever had in Asia. "But that made no difference. I had been overcome with a burning interest in coffee culture."

In recent years, coffee has elbowed its way into tea culture in China, giving it the potential to transform one of the world's smallest markets into its largest. When I first came to China in 2001, it was more or less impossible to find a decent cup of coffee. Back then, Starbucks was slowly starting to roll out its first cafés in China, but they were rare and mainly located in congested tourist areas. Today there are twice as many Starbucks shops in Shanghai as there are in New York City. Mann Li is feeding off the city's growing appetite for coffee, although with a somewhat more concentrated approach. His plan is to expand by one or two new cafes every year. He's also running a small barista school where he teaches other coffee buffs how to make the perfect cuppa, or even set up their own cafés. He acknowledges that by teaching people to run cafés, he's planting the seeds of upcoming competition. "Hey, at the end of they day we can all succeed. I see other cafés as colleagues, not competitors", he says.

He strikes a slightly surprising note of caution, however. "If you want to make money, do not open a cafe," he says. "I am doing this because I love coffee. It is an incredibly tough job, but also a great way of life."

Mann Li's ethos – that business is not just about money – is actually typical of the new generation in Shenzhen. Where the previous generation worked hard and saved for the future, younger people have much less reverence for money, reflecting a similar trend in many part of the West.

Older generations were raised to cherish lifetime employment and the stability of a large organization. But millennials in China, as elsewhere, are embracing gig work, part-time opportunities and entrepreneurialism. Co-working spaces and entrepreneurship are booming, and more and more foreigners are flooding in.

Shenzhen is undeniably a magnet for talents. So many graduates from all over China flock to the city that they make up a greater share of its population than do graduates in Beijing or Shanghai. About 20 percent of all China's PhDs live and work here, according to some estimates. The city also attracts high numbers of so called returnees, Chinese citizens who have studied and spent extended periods in places such as the United States and Europe, with some experts claiming that Shenzhen is the country's key beneficiary of China's overseas studies program.

So much has happened over these last four decades that the city has outsized many European countries in terms of population and economy. Today, according to official government numbers, 12 million people call Shenzhen home. Local officials often claim the real number is in fact over 20 million. (Some 4 million people have official hukou household registration, another 8 million have permanent residency, and 5-8 million "float" unofficially within the city). That's twice as many people as live in my native Sweden. It has also become one of the wealthiest cities in China: from 1979 to 2011, Shenzhen's average annual GDP growth rate was a staggering 25 percent. In 2016, its economy continued to outperform the national average and its GDP hit 1.95 trillion yuan ($284 billion), up 9 percent year-on-year. That's about the same size as the GDP of Denmark or the Philippines.

Some local officials are gutsy enough to state that the city owes its success not to the central government or the Communist Party but to its policy of allowing people to go "beyond the planned economy". Shenzhen was the pioneer, the wedge that helped shape modern urban life in all of the country. It became the poster city and, above all, a shining example of a modern China that works.

Indeed, when China's president Xi Jinping launched the idea of the "Chinese dream" as a way to modernize the country's economy from low level manufacturing to a high-tech and service sector-based model, that dream was already in full bloom in Shenzhen. The city already invests more than 4 percent of its GDP annually in research and development, double the mainland average and on a par with South Korea and Israel. Most of the money comes from private firms.

In spite of its young age, Shenzhen's success is undeniable:

- It has the fourth largest local economy in the country. Its Nanshan district, home to about 125 listed firms with a combined market value of nearly $400bn, has a higher income per person than Hong Kong.

- Almost half of China's international patent applications are filed by Shenzhen companies, according to the Economist. In fact, firms in Shenzhen file more international patents – which are mostly of a higher quality than other Chinese ones – than companies in either France or Britain.

- Innovation-driven sectors such as biotechnology, ICT and new energy represent 40 percent of Shenzhen's economy, higher than any other city in China.

• Shenzhen is ranked by PwC as number one in China in terms of technology readiness, economic influence and ease of doing business.

• Shenzhen has surpassed Hong Kong as China's most competitive region thanks to innovation.

What's more, Shenzhen has the country's second largest stock exchange, the world's third-busiest container port and the fourth-busiest airport on the Chinese mainland. It's rolling out the world's largest metro line system and is soon set to have world's first all-electric public bus fleet. This single city currently builds more skyscrapers per year than the United States and Australia combined. The head of Invest Shenzhen, Wang Youming, calls it "a city of miracles".

Shenzhen has never hidden its ambition to become Asia's answer to Silicon Valley. In many areas it's already ahead.

HARDWARE PARADISE IN 'THE SILICON DELTA'

Edith Yeung is a general partner of 500 Startups, an early-stage venture fund and seed accelerator headquartered in Silicon Valley. She leans back in her chair, preparing to choose her words carefully. I have just asked her how she would explain Shenzhen to an American or European investor who has never heard of the Chinese city.

"I would tell them it's a Silicon Valley for hardware", she says.

We meet in Hong Kong, during the largest and most exciting startup conference in Asia, Rise. Here, zillions of enthusiastic startups mingle, bumping elbows for a few minutes talking to global media, investors or potential partners who have flown in to size up the latest trends and opportunities. On several stages, CEO and VC luminaries share their wisdom and opinions, while the media room is abuzz with interviews in sundry different languages. Part of the conference involves a visit across the border to Shenzhen to witness the city "where China's transformation began". Many of the participating firms and speakers are based in Shenzhen, and many more have a manufacturing base there. In a polling station at the event guests are asked "Will China overtake Silicon Valley?" and requested to place stickers according to their view. A majority of the stickers are in the circle saying "yes".

Generally, says Yeung, Americans still see the US as the center of the universe and have a limited understanding of what's happening on the Chinese tech scene. At the same time, she adds, young Chinese readily follow and absorb international trends and news.

Head of her firm's China unit, which has invested in several startups here, she says: "Americans have no idea what's going on in China. There are so many areas where China already exceeds the US."

Comparing the situation in Shenzhen with the ecosystem in Silicon Valley, Yeung says that where many in the Valley work for big companies like Facebook, Google or Apple for some years before leaving to create their own startups, here they spend time at giants such as DJI, Tencent or Huawei then go off and set up their own shop.

A major difference is that people in Shenzhen have access to the world's most advanced supply chain for manufacturing and distribution. Shenzhen is surrounded by several satellite cities, such as Dongguan, Huizhou and Zhongshan, which together form a complete supply chain providing almost everything from raw materials to computer components at low cost.

Industry clusters in China are more powerful than most Westerners understand. Although I myself travel through these areas and write about tech issues regularly, I still find it difficult to get my head around the sheer scale of what I see. Driving through the Delta – from Guangzhou in the north to Hong Kong in the south – takes about four hours. During those four hours, the urban landscape never stops. There is no such thing as countryside here. The highways wind through uninterrupted urban sprawl. The World Bank recently declared the Delta the world's biggest megacity, surpassing Tokyo, and some 60 million people call it their home. That's a population roughly the same as Britain's.

Though the Pearl River Delta region accounts for less than 1 percent of China's territory and 5 percent of its population, it generates more than a tenth of its GDP and a quarter of its exports. It soaks up a fifth of China's total foreign direct investment and has attracted over a trillion dollars in foreign direct investments since 1980. Shenzhen is at the heart of what the Economist calls "the Silicon Delta".

Unlike other technology clusters in China that are focused on the domestic market, Shenzhen and its Delta serve the world and so have an infrastructure designed mainly for exports and global business.

Shenzhen will also be at the heart of the Greater Bay Area, a government-initiated "super economic zone" weaving Hong Kong, Macau and other cities in Guangdong even closer economically and socially. The project is being championed by Premier Li Keqiang and aims to create a world-class technology hub based on increased cooperation in the region. Think Hong Kong's finance + Shenzhen's innovation + Guangdong's manufacturing. And on top of that, you can add a bit of gambling and leisure in Macao. The scheme to link eleven cities in the south into one economic hub could produce a region with an economy about the size of South Korea's (the fourth largest economy in Asia and the 11th largest in the world) if it were made a free-trade zone, according to some estimates.

For Yeung it's a no-brainer. With all its advantages, market players just can't ignore Shenzhen.

"Shenzhen has a very clear personality and proposition in terms of how to add value on hardware stuff," she says. "Worldwide, everybody needs to go there. If you haven't been there you're missing something. A lot of local Chinese are super amazing at producing hardware and I see a lot of investment opportunities. There are already amazing companies that came from Shenzhen, and we will see more."

She adds: "If you're not already in Shenzhen, you're crazy."

Now, it's clear that more and more multinationals – perhaps wary of seeming crazy – are taking increasing advantage of the region's skills, not just in manufacturing but in research and development too. Last year, Apple announced that it would open a research center in Shenzhen to tap the local talent pool for writing computer software. And, just recently, Airbus – the world's largest plane maker – selected Shenzhen for its China innovation center, with Luo Gang, head of the facility, explaining how "the city boasts global competitive advantages in technology research and development, industrialization, and international expansion."

Business magazine Inc puts it slightly differently: if you're interested in establishing a footprint in the world's most populous country, Shenzhen may well be your next home.

While there are still some significant downsides to doing business in China – from red tape and intellectual property theft to internet censorship – if you're a startup making a product you'll likely have trouble finding another city where you can manufacture your goods more cheaply and efficiently. People in Shenzhen have emerged as experts in how to enlarge factory production efficiently; they are pragmatic and have real experience in making and manufacturing. Working from Shenzhen makes it easier to work out technical problems by liaising directly with suppliers. Besides, the city is home to almost 15,000 logistics companies, and over 80 percent of China's supply chain management companies are headquartered here.

Jixun Foo, managing partner of GGV Capital, also hails Shenzhen's ecosystem for smart hardware. GGV Capital is a multi-stage investor specializing in American and Chinese startups. Foo has been involved in some of the country's most spectacular mergers and acquisitions (including the first billion dollar tech M&A in China, for Youku Tudou). He's been recognized by Forbes China as one of the "Best Venture Capitalists" every year for the last decade.

Today, GGV has investments in two Shenzhen-based firms: Headphone maker 1More, and Immotor, which makes electric scooters with a patented super battery. Both firms are being praised in tech media for providing clever solutions to everyday issues. Foo also manages the firm's Shenzhen-based venture AAC Technologies, a supplier of acoustic components for handheld devices including the iPhone. Floated on the Hong Kong stock exchange in 2005, it's now the largest acoustics supplier in the world, he tells me. In our interview, Foo talks at lengths about both his own firms' and Shenzhen's hardware ecosystems.

"Shenzhen is a hotspot for talents," he says. "Five years from now, Shenzhen will continue to build on these strengths."

His view on the future of Shenzhen is clear: if you believe in robotics, driverless cars and smart machines, this is the place to be. The reason for this, he says, lies in the combination of young creative people and the city's unique access to the supply chain. For both Chinese and international companies in hardware and robotics, he says, Shenzhen will be the natural place to be over the coming years.

"The next generation of smart vehicles, you'll see them coming out of south China because of the whole supply chain that is there. It's a very important factor," Foo says.

"The next ten years will be the era of robots and intelligent machines, and Shenzhen will play well to that and capitalize on the trend."

As an example, he mentions electric carmaker BYD (an acronym derived from the phrase "build your dreams"), one of the world's largest producers of electric cars and batteries. In many ways it's like a Chinese Tesla – only better at peddling cars. The Shenzhen-based automaker sold more than 100,000 vehicles in 2016; in comparison, Tesla delivered only 76,000. There has been an amusing gunslinger stand-off between Tesla's founder Elon Musk, who has mocked BYD for substandard technology, and BYD founder Wang Chuanfu, who reportedly once told his investors that BYD could build a car like a Tesla "in a few minutes". Some investors seem to listen to the Chinese entrepreneur: His company is backed by Warren Buffett's Berkshire Hathaway.

When I ask Jixun Foo if he thinks Shenzhen has an advantage over Silicon Valley, he doesn't hesitate.

"Absolutely! There's no supply chain in the US that has migrated out over the last few decades in the same way. The very basic costs of building a machine – the turn-around plan, prototyping, innovation – are a lot lower in China today, especially for hardware innovation. There's a lot of intellectual power in Silicon Valley, a lot of things like artificial intelligence and virtual reality are being developed there, but the power and strength of China is that the cost of adoption, prototyping and innovation is low."

China is already the world's biggest spender on industrial robots and a global leader in automation, according to the International Federation of Robotics (IFR), and the Pearl River Delta seems to play well to this trend. According to

Invest Shenzhen – which may, admittedly, be slightly biased – the city's companies are national leaders in everything from systems integration, multi-sensor fusion and signal processing to person-machine interaction. China is also speeding ahead in the race to be global leader in artificial intelligence. It plans to make the AI industry a central economic growth driver and to globally dominate in the production of semiconductors, autonomous vehicles, biotechnology and other high-tech sectors. Goldman Sachs recently issued a report saying China has emerged as a major global contender in using AI to drive economic progress, and concluded that the country has the talent, data and infrastructure needed to fully embrace AI. There is a massive amount of money flowing into innovation in artificial intelligence in China. Shenzhen's local government supports the advancement of AI and is offering grants of US$1 million to help AI companies or projects set up there.

In a busy office in High-Tech Park, I meet the founders of Sennotech, a startup firm which makes smart insoles. The product is basically a portable gait analysis system that uses advanced algorithms to collect and monitor data about a wearer's feet. This data, and analysis thereof, can help people correct walking problems, and also help to detect if an individual is at risk of stroke or other morbidities.

"We are best in the world on what we are doing", says Qin Li, who started the firm with his friend Zhinan Li. Both obtained their PhD or MS degrees in top-ranked European and US universities. "Our ambition is to be world leader in our segment."

Qin Li believes that Shenzhen has an advantage over Silicon Valley in all areas that involve manufacturing, including Internet of Things solutions, robotics and AI-integrated products.

"Shenzhen is just better that Silicon Valley in terms of hardware and software integration. Lots of Silicon Valley guys come here for initial R&D and demo products. Around Shenzhen is a full supply chain from material to design to production," he says. "Shenzhen is also a place for innovation consciousness and open minded people. These were the two factors that attracted us."

If venture capital activity is any indicator, the city is on the right track. Today, China is among the top three markets in the world for VC investment in digital technology, including virtual reality, autonomous vehicles, 3D printing, robotics, drones and AI, according to a 2017 McKinsey report that highlights the unique advantages of Shenzhen: "China is already more digitized than many observers appreciate and has the potential to set the world's digital frontier in coming decades," it says. "China's digital players enjoy the notable advantage of close links to hardware manufacturers. The Pearl River Delta industrial hub is likely to continue to be a major producer of connected devices because of its strength in manufacturing hardware."

Jeffrey Towson, a private equity investor and Peking University professor – and also the co-writer of the brilliant One Hour China books – stresses the unique advantages of Shenzhen's innovation and its Delta supply chain.

"In terms of hardware plus software innovation, Shenzhen is ahead of the curve. Silicon Valley innovates mostly in software. But China can do both and they tend to be better in smart devices, drones and other combinations of manufacturing and software," he tells me in an interview.

Speaking of digitalization and how the society is rapidly changing, another cool thing about Shenzhen (and most other Chinese cities) is that no one is using cash anymore. From the small shops at the electronic market and your local dumpling restaurant to factories and travel agents, all have embraced mobile phone payment apps as their main means of payment. Even the vendors of counterfeit watches and bags by the Hong Kong border crossing accept mobile payments.

In fact, a recent study showed that Chinese consumers spend about 50 times more through mobile payment platforms than their American counterparts.

I remembered this one morning when I was standing in line at a Starbucks in downtown Shenzhen and suddenly realized that no one in front of me was paying with cash. They weren't using credit cards either. In fact, I couldn't see a single customer holding a wallet or a purse. Instead, they just held their mobile phones over a reader and – beep! – the latte was theirs. "Almost no one uses cash here anymore," cafe manager Lily Li told me, adding that more than 80 percent of all payments in the coffee shop are made via mobile phones. I almost felt embarrassed holding out a wrinkly, dirty old bill as payment.

The same day I saw two women on the street selling noodles from a small stall during the morning rush. Amid the steam billowing from the big boiler and the smell of hot spices, I could hear the constant beeping of phones scanning the stall's QR code.

Among the country's 750 million internet users – more than the United States and Europe combined – the utilization ratio of mobile online payments is 68 percent. That can be compared with only 15 percent in the United States, according to a report by McKinsey Global Institute.

Shenzhen has been ranked China's second smartest city in terms of going cashless, with Beijing being number one. A staggering 84 percent of polled Chinese consumers say they feel comfortable without carrying cash around because they have their mobile phones.

Some companies are already experimenting with shop concepts where consumers don't actively pay at all – you just pick whichever groceries you want and walk out. A camera recognizes your face and the stuff you've put in the basket, and takes money from your mobile wallet. Easy.

"Few foreigners realize how fast and advanced the development actually is in new payment features and mobile financial services in China," says Mofei Chen, founder and CEO of Shenzhen-based Money Bazaar, a peer-to-peer currency exchange platform. "I can hardly remember the last time I used my wallet."

Our interview takes place at SimplyWork, a shared office in one of the city's tech parks. Here, hardware and software startups blend with e-commerce and venture capital firms. Young entrepreneurs can be seen lying on sofas with laptops on their bellies, while others are having animated conversations in small groups. Toys and skateboards are strewn across the floor, and fluffy pet dogs and cats are playing under the tables. Enthusiasm and creativity abound. At the entrance of the co-working space a sign says: "No stupid people beyond this point." I can't help but think that the same sign might just as well have been placed at the city's border.

HARDWARE ACCELERATORS CONNECTING THE WORLD

Shenzhen has received increased attention in international media, often with thundering superlatives being used to describe the transformation from "sleepy fishing village" to "Asia's Silicon Valley". In a widely quoted special report on the Silicon Delta by The Economist, the magazine stated that "Shenzhen has done more than any place on the mainland to debunk the outdated myth of 'copycat China', becoming the global hub of innovation in hardware and manufacturing."

I also enjoyed how Scott Edmunds, a former Shenzhen resident who edits a biotech journal, nailed it when he – in a Nature interview – described the city as "a bit of a nerd's paradise. If you're a tech nerd, it's heaven."

But the most important questions for any newcomer to Shenzhen must be: How do I tap into this? And where do I start? Believe me, it can be quite daunting. During my first visit to the city I was totally overwhelmed by the magnitude and pure size of the place. I mean, it has twice as many people as my native Sweden. I got lost. I felt lost. And it took me several trips, and some guidance from local friends, to get to know my way around.

A first good step is to reach out to any of the international accelerators, incubators or maker spaces. You can also contact Invest Shenzhen, although they are far from quick in replying to emails. In Hong Kong and Guangzhou you will also get great support from countries' chambers of commerce or general-consulates. Invest Hong Kong is also a great – and very welcoming – recourse for the entire Greater Bay Area. Specialized consultancy firms, such as Kaizor Innovation, offer guided tours through the city. For me personally, some of Shenzhen's many co-working spaces have been a gold mine for connecting with local startups, especially SimplyWork (mentioned in the last chapter) which has around ten locations across town.

Some accelerators are doing an amazing job in connecting foreign startups with local counterparts and helping entrepreneurs to get their feet on the ground. The most famous is called HAX.

Cyril Ebersweiler, a general partner at SOSV, a venture capital firm recently ranked the most active global seed investor by TechCrunch, set up the HAX Accelerator in an office space in the heat of the buzzing Huaqiangbei technology market in 2011. As described earlier, the area is famous for two things: tech gadgets, and components to build your own tech gadgets. What could be better for a bunch of hardware geeks?

The idea of HAX – which, with over 200 investments in five years, has been ranked the world's most active hardware investor – is to select startups from around the world with good product ideas, and invite them to spend 111 days in Shenzhen. Here, with the help of a team of 30 people, they refine their strategy and explore how to turn their prototypes into actual products which could be manufactured at scale. They are surrounded by dozens of other HAX startups, including alumni who are farther along, some having run million-dollar campaigns on Kickstarter. The accelerator also has a follow-up program in San Francisco to help teams grow by focusing on sales and marketing. "When building hardware all roads leads to Shenzhen", it says on its website.

The reason for picking this location in Huaqiangbei, Ebersweiler explains, was to get access to the city's low-priced materials and lightning-fast manufacturers. Basically, it's an ideal playground for hardware start-ups to build prototypes and move into production, he says, acknowledging that the city has developed its own unique rules and skills.

"With a good understanding of foreign practices and the proximity with Hong Kong for international travel purposes, Shenzhen is the right place to be," he says.

The most reaffirming moment came, he remembers, when, one day, the founder of a startup in the accelerator program, Particle, ordered a micro-controller online, and it turned out that the office selling it was just one floor down in the same building. They were prototyping within the hour.

Another example is Voltera, a company formerly based in San Francisco that makes circuit-board 3D printers. Shortly after getting onto HAX's program the company moved to Shenzhen to take control of its supply chain and manufacturing base. "There is no better place to be than the electronics capital of the world", the firm's co-founder, Alroy Almeida, says in a video posted online.

Benjamin Joffe, a partner at HAX, explains that Silicon Valley's understanding of hardware is "six to seven years out of date".

"Many startups and investors in the Valley have an outdated perception of how hardware startups are built," he says. "They think it's slow, expensive, and difficult. Today, many hardware startups need less capital and less time to get to market. It is still harder than a mobile app but that's also a defense against competitors. I would say hardware in 2017 is comparable in difficulty and cost to pre-cloud websites, when you had to operate your own servers."

He adds that the combination of software with hardware opens the door to a new "steam engine time" – with sensors, AI, machine learning and robotics all getting to grips with the physical world. Every industry is involved, from healthcare to agriculture and mining, he says.

Most of the city's accelerators and co-working spaces are located in hyper modern technology parks. Massive glittering skyscrapers tower up along the broad boulevards. Well-dressed young professionals pedal along on colorful bicycles from bike-sharing companies, and electrical cars slowly swoosh by. It's like a parallel world to the city's old industrial areas.

At the launch of a new technology business incubator in one of these tech parks, I meet Luming Zhou, a government official turned tech accelerator boss. For 20 years, he worked for the Chinese government and was responsible for turning Shenzhen into a hub for high-tech firms, an achievement for which he is now known as the "Father of Tech Startups".

Zhou realized that working for the government didn't bring his vision forward fast enough or resourcefully enough, however. Unsatisfied, he left his official position and instead founded China Radical Innovation, an incubator for firms in sectors such as e-commerce, digital health and IT security. Broadly speaking, incubators and accelerators like these are businesses that help startups advance their development quickly, in whatever ways may be necessary: from mentoring to finding partners, either locally or globally, and helping them pitch their ideas to investors.

"The government is poor at making market-oriented decisions," he says. "So I quit in order to better bring together innovation among entrepreneurs."

The opening event at China Radical Innovation is a hive of activity. Enthusiastic young pioneers mingle with investors, corporate executives and local politicians. Champagne and chocolate delicacies are in abundance, but one group from a health tech startup company are glued to their screens trying to finish a project. Quotes from famous thinkers ranging from Salvador Dali to Steve Jobs cover the walls. (Actually, most co-working spaces in Shenzhen – and other Chinese cities – all have the same clichés on their walls).

Zhou explains how reforms in China are a step-by-step process and that Shenzhen is often used as a testing ground. Developments that are banned in other places in China are allowed here, he says. The bureaucracy is far more flexible than in other places. The city imposes relatively few limits on freedom of movement, is relaxed about employment contracts and does not discriminate against outsiders.

"It's easier to commercialize intellectual property rights here, such as innovations that have been developed at state universities," he says. "That has been encouraged by the central government. You see, here is where we build the Chinese dream."

MAKER SUBCULTURE WITH CHINESE CHARACTERISTICS

Shenzhen is home to a lively maker community, and it's one that also has its roots in Huaqiangbei and the Pearl River Delta's easy access to supplies. Makers are described as a contemporary subculture, representing a technology-based extension of do-it-yourself culture. The New York Times once called them "kitchen table industrialists."

One of my most memorable interviews on this topic was with a young female maker, or hardware hacker, in a tech-geek café called Vive in the city's High-tech Park district.

She's been called the world's sexiest hacker and she certainly lives up to that reputation. Naomi Wu, also known as SexyCyborg, is a 23-year-old Shenzhen native whose do-it-yourself videos have made her a global online phenomenon.

As she walks into a virtual reality gaming cafe in downtown Shenzhen wearing high leather boots, stay-up stockings, a pink miniskirt and tight top, she turns a fair number of heads. She's not shy of parading her 1,600cc of breast implants.

"When people see me in these clothes, they think I'm just a bimbo," Wu tells me as we sit down. "When they then realize that I do coding and tech stuff and make these videos, they go, 'Wow! If she can do it, how hard can it be?'" She beams, and takes a sip from a cup of tea with a thick layer of cheese on top – a popular local drink.

Naomi Wu's videos range from step-by-step guides to setting up a 3D-printer to detailed demonstrations of how she creates high-tech wearables. They are largely meant to inspire young women to go into technology, to code and to promote China as a hub for creative technology. They've racked up hundreds of thousands of views on YouTube, Imgur, Reddit and elsewhere, earning her a reputation as a cyberpunk icon.

After shooting zombies in one of the cafe's VR simulators, we talk about how Wu joined the maker community and why she wants to inspire more women to go into technology. When asked why she initially got involved in tech, she explains that at first it was just a way to make a living but soon transformed into a passion.

"It can be frustrating when I hear people on international tech sites talk about China. They say all we can do is copy and stuff like that. That is, of course, always an issue, but we're all working hard to improve and be more innovative. I like to show off some simple projects to demonstrate that we have a creative culture here and that we are not all clones and robots. We have interesting, eccentric people just like any other country."

She offers an interesting example of how women are getting more involved in the tech scene in China. In the 3D printing community, she says, we are starting to see more women from a crafting and cosplay background. These women, who are already familiar with prop making, digital sewing machines and vinyl cutters, are now starting to use 3D printers.

"A lot of the men who buy 3D printers don't really have a use for them. For them, it's just a cool tech toy. They often end up just downloading Yoda heads and calibration prints without a clear use. Women are less interested in playing with the printers and are more project-focused, be it for gifts or holiday decorations. We're starting to see not just young cosplay women, but moms and homemakers without any technical background doing detailed YouTube tutorials on fairly advanced CAD software," she says.

Companies, large as small, would benefit from more actively tapping into the local maker community to access new designs and ways of making things on a shoestring budget, she says.

"It's a proven way to promote innovation and creativity," she states. "Shenzhen is good because it's so easy to get access to components and custom fabrication services for small or single orders. The turnaround time for both parts and services is fast."

Together we walk to her friend's maker space, SteamHead. The room is jam-packed with all kinds of tools, apparatus and cables, as well as 3D-printers and prototypes, and – of course – people busy designing or building stuff. The room reeks of creativity. The maker space and its cofounders, Benjamin "James" Simpson and Carrie Leung, a couple from San Francisco who left Silicon Valley to explore new ideas in Shenzhen, also offers maker classes for children. Here and there one can see small 3D-printed dinosaurs and other funny figures made by the kids.

The maker space concept originated in Silicon Valley as a grass-roots movement shaped by ecological considerations and community-mindedness. Their aim is to stimulate collaboration and empower individuals through providing a co-working place to experiment, share and network.

Today, however, California struggles to match Shenzhen's ecosystem of makers.

"What makes Shenzhen unique for maker entrepreneurs is the rapid prototyping. And because of reduced lead-times and ease of obtaining materials, we see a huge decrease in costs here. We are able to do projects for 10 dollars that in the US or elsewhere in the world would cost 100 dollars," Simpson says.

Simpson also says that Shenzhen is an ideal place for maker education. From his experience, parents here don't want their kids inheriting the jobs of their grandparents' generation, as suppliers of cheap goods for the rest of the world. Rather, he says, parents want to see their children succeed as creators, as members of a class of people who are able to design solutions to problems.

"That makes it an excellent location for maker education. We see the interest from the parents and the appetite from the kids. The raw materials and electronics are inexpensive, available and quick. Suddenly it's affordable to let kids play with electronics, break things and make mistakes."

China's central government has made the development of creative entrepreneurship a policy priority. Whilst visiting a maker space in Shenzhen in January 2015, Chinese Premier Li Keqiang stressed that: "Maker spaces fully demonstrate the vitality, entrepreneurship and innovation, which will be the driver of Chinese economic growth in the future."

Is it any surprise that the largest maker fair in Asia – and the fourth largest in the world – is hosted in Shenzhen?

Maker spaces in China are, however, different from

ones in the West. Many of the major maker spaces here are supported by incubators, which are, in turn, backed by property tycoons or industrial giants, and have moneymaking rather than primarily social aspirations.

Philippe Kern, head of KEA International, a research center on cultural and creative industries with offices in Brussels and Shenzhen, believes that Shenzhen is an "ideal hotbed to encourage growth of creative entrepreneurship," partly based on its vibrant maker community. In an article on the organization's website he explains that the business model of most maker spaces is based on investment opportunities that successful future enterprises may generate.

He writes: "Maker spaces in Shenzhen are in effect large incubators (providing co-working space, mentoring, marketing and financial support) for young entrepreneurs with ideas. They concentrate on ICT hardware and software development (3D printing, robots, drones, connected equipment, mobile apps and internet of things). Their development and funding is supported by holding companies active in real estate, finance, construction or logistics. Such companies can nurture creative entrepreneurs, provide business training, seed funding as well as investment capital at later development stage.

"In effect, the strength of Shenzhen's maker spaces lies in the integration of strong financial investment capacity to fund new businesses. This will make Shenzhen attractive to creative professionals worldwide looking for capital funding and affordable manufacturing."

Either way, for international companies and investors it's absolutely worth paying a visit to any of these maker spaces. And I would say the same thing about the many co-working spaces, where you'll find an abundance of fascinating startups. (As mentioned before, send an email to shenzhensuperstars@gmail.com with subject FREE GIFT and I'll send you a list of accelerators, co-working and marker spaces and tech parks).

LESSONS FROM TECH PIRATES

The maker community and hardware startup scene remain, even today, connected to another highly interesting, although controversial, part of the city's story. Aside from being the world's hardware haven for legal stuff, the Pearl River Delta – and perhaps especially the Huaqiangbei commercial area – is famous for something else: tech pirates.

But wait. Don't brush them off quite yet. There's more to these rip-off artists than one might think, and they have much to teach Western businesses in terms of supply chain management, design and trend spotting. Many counterfeit companies are partly a result of factory engineers quitting their jobs making products for foreign brands, and instead applying their acquired knowledge to make cheaper – and sometimes better – reproductions or adaptations. The Chinese word for counterfeiters is shanzhai, which literally means "mountain village" or "mountain stronghold" and refers to the mountain stockades of regional warlords or bandits, far away from official control. Shenzhen's counterfeit entrepreneurs indeed have a nose for what's hot and what's not, and for how to quickly bring a product to market and make a pile of cash. Behind the façade of this murky trade is a sophisticated network of R&D, sales and logistics.

A Finnish professor of innovation, design and management at the University of Southern Denmark, Alf Rehn, once told a story at a conference in Stockholm about how he had spend time with a Chinese bicycle enthusiast who made a living from making and selling rip-offs of the Italian bicycle brand Bianchi. One year when Bianchi launched a new model, this guy was disappointed with the quality of the original and decided to improve on it. The copy model he put on the market did not only cost a fraction of the price of the original, but boasted higher functionality and quality.

This is just one of many examples of how, through constantly tweaking and testing knockoffs, the industry has ended up producing upgraded visions – such as an iPhone with space for three SIM cards – and even inventing entirely new products that can be exported around the world. Some commentators actually believe that shanzhai is a powerful force behind Shenzhen's design success. The design magazine Metropolis recently stated: "The flagrant abuse of intellectual property rights at Huaqiangbei, while infuriating many, has garnered sympathy from a global community of makers who have been championing notions of open-source sharing, Creative Commons licensing, and innovation through iteration for over a decade."

As part of my research for various feature stories I've come in contact with many counterfeiters, from executives for large manufacturers to consultants specializing in the logistics of forgeries. It's quite exciting. I have several good anecdotes, but I will limit myself to two. The first one is about how pirates profited from the Apple subsidiary Beats by Dr. Dre; the other is about how they brutally turned a cold shoulder to a famous tech brand, Samsung Galaxy Gear.

I wrote the story about Beats by Dr. Dre headphones for CNN just as hip-hop star Andre Young – better known as Dr. Dre – become the world's top money-making musician and his Beats Electronics line reached a record valuation. But the former N.W.A. rapper was not the only one profiting from his headphone line. Across the Pearl River Delta in southern China, counterfeit Beats were flowing out of factories, assembly workshops and shops, attracting middlemen who sell the headphones on global markets.

I approached wholesale companies about buying in bulk in order to learn how the underground sale of knock-off headphones works. I said I was a consultant.

"Business is very good," said a woman, who, with her family, runs a wholesale company selling copied headphones in one of Shenzhen's many mega-malls. "You buy cheap from me, you sell expensive in your home country, we all make a lot of money."

To prove her point, she showed me an Excel spreadsheet on her laptop listing customers from all over the world: Italy, Denmark, the United States, Canada, Dubai, Russia and more. She said she recently sold a large shipment of counterfeit Beats by Dr. Dre for $50,000 to a British businessman who had them sent to the UK by jet – which is considerably more expensive than container ship – and sold them as originals.

Behind the shops and inside small rooms around the district, I could see workers in their early 20s busily assembling counterfeit goods such as smartphones and iPads. The long corridors were filled with cigarette smoke drifting out from tiny workshops as deliverymen rushed by with their arms full of electronic components. Everywhere you could hear the sound of packing tape being wrapped around cardboard boxes.

At another Shenzhen store, a sales executive for a factory and trading company connected a fake pair of Beats Pro to her iPhone and put them on my head. The sound quality was surprisingly good. In the US, an original pair would cost $400. She offers her best quality headphones for the wholesale price of $70, medium quality for $45 and "so-so quality" for $30.

"Medium quality is most popular, but the trend is going towards high-end. Consumers want good sound," she said, adding that she can deliver 100 units of any Beats product by the following day. For 1,000 items it will take a week. "Since it's copies, we don't want to have too much in stock."

I also spoke with another woman involved in the trade – a "copy brand exports professional" according to her business card – who helps companies to transport counterfeit goods from Shenzhen to other countries. She said she advises her customers to avoid Chinese logistic companies and always use European or American shipping companies since "customs usually trusts these brands better."

Store owners reveal other tricks to bypass customs. They send all Beats in two boxes; the outer box has a made-up name to hide the real goods.

Precautions aside, in the Huaqiangbei commercial district few seem to have any moral objections about the pirating of goods. Outside the Huaqiangbei Police Station, a friendly officer in sunglasses points down the street when asked where the best fake mobile phones can be found. Asked if such purchases are legal, he just breaks out in loud laughter.

If Beats by Dr. Dre rip-offs were a success for the Shenzhen pirates, Samsung's Galaxy Gear smartwatch was initially a disaster – at least for the Korean maker of the original.

When the smartwatch first launched – accompanied by a humongous advertising campaign – I was curious to know what the counterfeiters' in Shenzhen thought about the company's hyped wearable gadgets. Again, I approached wholesale companies and retailers at the world's biggest electronics trading districts.

Interestingly, the pirates gave Samsung's wearable technology the cold shoulder.

"There are no copies for sale. Only originals," said the managing director of a wholesale company that specializes in mobile electronic devices. "Maybe we'll have fakes in a few months. I don't know, interest is low."

Out of 20 shops I visited, not one sold fake Samsung Gear smartwatches and none could offer leads on where to find copies.

What is the lesson here? China's thriving market for counterfeit electronic goods has been a headache for global hi-tech firms including Apple, Microsoft and Nikon, as illegal cut-price copies of much sought-after products eat into their profits. But, one might argue, if there is one thing worse than being copied, that is to be ignored.

The lack of copy versions of the Gear is a "serious warning signal," according to professor and provocateur Alf Rehn, who has spent years studying the global piracy phenomena.

"Piracy is all about benefiting from buzz – create something good enough that looks like the real deal, and make money off those who are not willing or able to pay for the authentic item but who still want to be 'with it.'

"Without the buzz, there's no need for the counterfeit. So this isn't necessarily a disaster for Samsung, but definitively a serious warning signal as the Shenzhen crowd is the bellwether for electronics consumption."

It's not uncommon for top-selling products to be on the market before the launch of the original. Likewise, unpopular products are unceremoniously dropped by pirates who simply cannot afford to get stuck with the inventory. According to Rehn, there are stories about how new Nokia models were basically discontinued by counterfeiters before the genuine article even made it to market.

"This is a warp-speed market economy, where every product faces an 'up or out' decision on a daily basis. Competition is brutal," Rehn adds.

HUAWEI,
THE HARDWARE PIONEER

There are tons of interesting companies from Shenzhen I could have used to illustrate the uniqueness of the city. But if there is one company that can symbolize its journey from a dirty factory town to a tech nerd heaven, that is Huawei. Founded in a small apartment three decades ago, it has grown into by far the world's biggest telecom giant. Through the years the company and the city have walked hand in hand, from being peddlers of low-quality hardware to global innovation frontrunners. As Shenzhen has grown, so has Huawei. They both embody the rise of modern China.

"It's interesting to look at both Huawei and Shenzhen in parallel because the sheer rate of growth of Shenzhen and the sheer globalization of Shenzhen has kind of happened in parallel with this fast growth and globalization for Huawei", says Joe Kelly, the company's global corporate communications leader.

I meet Kelly during a visit to the company's gigantic campus in Shenzhen. Walking through it is like entering a parallel world; one inhabited by well-dressed young engineers and office workers with keycards around their necks. The corridors are lined with restaurants serving all kinds of international cuisine. There are several 7-Elevens, hotels and a sports club with a swimming pool. There's a Huawei university where new employees undergo a three-month familiarization course. Some 10,000 people live in the campus dormitories. There's even a small lake, complete with a family of black swans.

In one of the labs I meet a young woman who is, quite literally, butchering mobile phones. Twenty-four-year-old Qin Shengni works as a test engineer and is pressing, hitting and scrubbing handsets to trial their quality. She's using a variety of apparatuses and tools.

"The company is very strict when it comes to quality", she tells me, and she does not sound like she's repeating PR quotes but rather like she really believes in her chores.

Her job, however, is not just to put handsets through the wringer and make sure they meet international standards, but – perhaps more importantly – to find ways of improving quality and usability.

"As engineers we are allowed to make mistakes, but not to repeat them. The management wants us to explore new possibilities, learn new things and share our experiences with everybody who works here. It's a very creative environment", she says before going back to tormenting the devices.

The story of Huawei is the story of its founder, Ren Zhengfei. Born in 1944 into a rural family, Ren spent his childhood years in a remote, mountainous town in Guizhou Province. After university he joined the People's Liberation Army (PLA) research institute as a military technologist. Then, in 1987, at the age of 44, he founded Huawei Technologies Co. Ltd in a small apartment in Shenzhen.

When launched, the firm had start-up capital of just 21,000 yuan, ($3,100 in today's money) in registered capital. Its employees, both managers and employees, worked in the apartment, which also served as a kitchen and dormitory. The level of innovation was initially meager and the firm mostly re-sold telephone exchange equipment imported from Hong Kong. Working conditions were poor. Its slogan was: "Let us drink to celebrate success, but if we fail, let's fight tooth and nail to come out alive."

It all happened in a time and a place in Chinese history that were as unique as they were chaotic. In the early days of the country's reforms, Huawei was sometimes dismissed as a "bastard of a business", according to a book about the company, and Ren was portrayed as a delusional Don Quixote, lance in hand, tilting at windmills with unrealistic dreams. It was a time of both confusion and opportunities, and Ren did the most with what history offered.

Slowly, the firm outgrew the turmoil and climbed in the value chain with its own innovations and products. Today, Huawei's products and services are available in more than 170 countries, and are used by a third of the world's population.

A few years ago, a reporter from the Wall Street Journal asked John Chamber, CEO of Cisco Systems, "Which company worries you the most among all your competitors?" Chamber replied without hesitation, "Very simple – 25 years ago, I already knew that my biggest rival would be from China. Now I can see it is Huawei."

The world's biggest telecoms-equipment vendor, Huawei is now also a major force in both smartphones and cloud computing. Ten years ago, Sweden's Ericsson was world leader in telecoms and twice the size of Huawei. Today Huawei is almost three times the size of Ericsson.

Huawei spends more on research and development than Apple does. Almost half of its 170,000 employees are in research and development. Sixteen R&D centers have been set up in the United States, Germany, Sweden, Russia, India, and China. This innovation-driven environment has made Huawei the most popular employer for young university graduates in the country. In a ranking by Universum, Huawei tops the technology category and take second place in the business category.

Undeniably, the story of Huawei further testifies to the triumph of Deng Xiaoping's opening-up policies. A book about the company, called Huawei: Leadership, Culture and Connectivity, says the company would not have survived the 1980s had it not been based in Shenzhen.

During my visit to the campus, Joe Kelly reaffirms that being located in the Shenzhen and Pearl River Delta region has benefited the company, and likewise the region has benefited from having a major tech player as Huawei here. He explains how the company's supply chain for smartphones is contained within the cities surrounding Shenzhen, in Guangdong province, and how the company takes advantage of the ecosystem and pool of talents that exist in the region, not only in Shenzhen itself but in the cities nearby.

And he believes the growth story of the city is still speeding up.

"I think it will continue. And I think the biggest change that people see is in the reputation of Shenzhen. You know, today we all think about Silicon Valley. In the last year I've seen more and more people saying: 'Wow, this is China's Silicon Valley'. I do think that this will become more of a story. And as it becomes more of a story, it will continue to fuel the development of Shenzhen", he says.

TENCENT,
THE SOFTWARE ARMY KNIFE

Apart from Huawei, I'd like to put forward one more case study: Tencent.

The story of Tencent and its CEO and co-founder Pony Ma is a typical Shenzhen story. It's also an inspiring tale of how an insignificant internet company became one of the largest internet service portals in world. And it highlights the fact that Shenzhen is not just about hardware, but also software. And honestly, it's impossible to write about Shenzhen without writing about this Tencent.

For anyone who hasn't heard of the company, imagine a Swiss army knife where each tool is a unique tech service. One tool resembles WhatsApp, another PayPal, others Google or Uber. Founded two decades ago, it is now among the most powerful forces in the global IT industry and its WeChat app is totally transforming daily life in China. At the time of writing, China's biggest tech company had just surpassed Facebook to become the fifth-largest internet company in the world by market capitalization.

"Tencent is the most interesting internet company in the world," says Jeffrey Towson, a private equity investor and Peking University professor.

My interview with Towson is conducted via WeChat, Tencent's flagship product. WeChat – or Weixin as it's called in China – has almost 1 billion monthly active users and totally dominates Chinese people's time online. But it's much more than a chat app. With its Wallet service you can pay for more or less anything in online and offline stores everywhere, top up your mobile phone, book flights, manage utility bills and even donate to charity. With its mini-apps you can hire a shared bicycle or a car. The app is also transforming businesses' online presence.

Recently I conducted an interview with an education technology company in Shenzhen. MasteRec has decided not to use a traditional website or develop its own app. Instead it is using WeChat as its only platform. On the ed-tech firm's WeChat page users can browse profiles, connect and communicate, and make bookings and payments. This means, basically, that Chinese businesses and individuals no longer need the World Wide Web to have an online platform. They can go straight to WeChat. The founder of the firm told me it was not just easier and cheaper to set up a WeChat platform than a normal internet webpage or app, but a better stage for connecting with clients.

No wonder. More than a third of its users spend in excess of four hours a day on the service. To put that in context, consider that the average person around the world spends a little more than an hour a day on Facebook, Instagram, Snapchat, and Twitter – combined.

"What strikes me as great about Tencent is how original they are. It's not a one-hit-wonder company like Facebook, PayPal and so many others. They keep hitting another ball over the fence every two to three years," Jeffrey Towson continues.

"I mean, what has Twitter developed over the last ten years? Or Facebook? It's still the same model. With Tencent we see new services and areas of investments constantly. They lead the way."

Not much is known about Tencent co-founder Pony Ma's early life. He grew up in Shantou in eastern Guangdong province, and when his father got a job as a port manager in Shenzhen the young Ma accompanied him. He graduated from Shenzhen University in 1993 with a Bachelor of Science degree in computer science and got his first job was with China Motion Telecom Development, where he reportedly earned $176 per month.

In 1998, at the age of 26, he co-founded Tencent in a cramped Shenzhen office with three college classmates and a friend. In the beginning, Ma is said to have performed various roles, ranging from janitor to website designer, in a bid to keep the company alive.

Just as in the case of Huawei, the initial days of Tencent were more about adaptation than innovation. Its first instant-messaging product, QQ, was essentially a copy of the Israeli system ICQ, tweaked for the Chinese market. In 2004, Tencent became the largest Chinese instant messaging service and went public. But after developing a reputation as a copycat, Ma decided to put the company through some institutional self-reflection. That make-over has paid off. Today it's China's king of patents. More than half of its staff belongs to the R&D department, and the firm has the country's biggest number of patent applications in areas including information search and database structure.

The cramped office where the founders kicked off is no more. Today, Tencent is headquartered in Shenzhen's Anshan district, in one of the city's most spectacular buildings, a bright and airy glass skyscraper designed by Seattle-based architecture firm NBBJ Design LLP. Some say the towers, linked by three angular skybridges, resemble giant, slow-dancing robots. The company has been ranked by Chinese students as one of the country's "most desirable employers."

The firm has become a global major strategic investor, with interests in everything from Tesla and several Silicon Valley health and biotech tech startups to Chinese investment banks and even space ventures. Few seem to know, but it's also the world's biggest gaming company.

Still, Ma remains publicity-shy and low-key and rarely appears in public. Colleagues and friends cited in a Bloomberg profile say he's a typical Guangdong province businessman, shy and wary of the spotlight. In a widely distributed photo, taken at a 2015 meeting of Chinese President Xi Jinping and 28 of the world's most famous technology executives – including Jeff Bezos, Tim Cook, and Jack Ma – everyone is smiling and looking at the camera.

Except for Pony Ma, who's staring at his feet.

ROOTLESSNESS, CLAMPDOWNS AND FAKE CSR

This short e-book mainly focuses on opportunities and possibilities. But living, working and doing business in China does, naturally, come with a bucketful of headaches. As a China correspondent, it's often the dark corners I tend to cover. I will raise just a few areas of concern.

There is an abundance of illegal factories in the Pearl River Delta and a tradition of faking corporate social responsibility (CSR) and labor condition certificates. Many of the satellite cities sounding Shenzhen are not experiencing anywhere near the same transformation into a modern economy and the situation sometimes gives rise to desperate measures. One way to lower manufacturing costs is to farm out production to illegal, unregulated small factories. Several people with whom I have spoken to confirm that this practice has become systematized in recent years.

A few years ago, together with a local friend in the neighboring city of Dongguan, I visited an area where dozens of dirty workshops sat side by side along both sides of the street. Manufacturing was underway inside the premises and even out on the sidewalk. One place was making shoes, another machines for making shoes; some were making furniture, others bags.

We enter one of the workshops. I have visited plenty of factories in my years in China but never any as downtrodden as this. The room looked like an aircraft hangar, only the corrugated sheet metal walls were gaping with huge holes and pockmarked with rust. The air was filled with dirt and tiny particles. A row of workers stood bent over in one corner wearing facemasks, grinding aluminum rods for chair frames. On the other side a woman sat assembling parts. The floor was strewn with aluminum chips and oil. The workers were so absorbed with their duties that no one reacted as I walked around taking photographs.

A European purchaser of accessories from well-known Western brands confirms the habit of faking CSR and labor condition certificates continues to grow in factory cities. It goes without saying, but as an investor or buyer in the Pearl River Delta you have to make sure to inspect manufacturing locations and also have independent inspectors covering your back. Even third party inspectors, however, are notorious for taking bribes in return for fake reports. Things can, and often do, get dirty.

"The bigger factories are farming out more and more of their production to smaller plants, often small workshops. We do not know what goes on in those places," the European purchaser admits. "The manufacturers' costs are rising quickly but we as buyers are not willing to pay more. So they have to find other ways of lowering costs."

A second area of concern is the lack of a functioning legal system. China still has a reputation – partly justified, partly exaggerated – for corruption, intellectual property theft and looting foreign joint ventures. Running a foreign entity in China has its fair share of red-tape complications, as well as unfair competition from local firms that are protected by discriminatory regulations and protectionism. The country unpredictable legal system is not based on the rule of law, some contend, but the rule-of-man.

I have heard several stories of European businessmen who

have had their Chinese companies or joint-ventures raided or looted by local partners, or have been lured into taking part in bribery and illegal activities to keep their factories running. One China manager for a major Swedish listed industrial company told me how he drives around with "a cardboard box full or cash" to pay off local suppliers.

Working behind the Great Firewall is also a constant annoyance. Ask anyone and they will give you an earful about slow internet speeds, blocked sites and VPN hassles. China operates one of the world's most sophisticated internet censorship systems, and was "the worst abuser of internet freedom" in 2016, according to a report by Freedom House. Both Google and Facebook, for example, are blocked here. So are many international news websites. Lack of freedom of speech and fear of government clampdowns are no doubt factors in stifling innovation, original thinking and willingness to break boundaries. Beijing's increased grip on freedoms has reportedly forced many Chinese academics to move abroad. Local startup founders I've spoken with say it would be disastrous for their businesses if they didn't have access to virtual private networks. But as anyone who has worked in China knows all too well, getting the VPN to work can be pure torture.

And you might wonder why there's no interview with Invest Shenzhen in this book. Well, the government organization is not allowed to speak with foreign journalists, a person working there told me.

I would also like to put the spotlight on another, often overlooked, source of distress: the impact of living in a city of constant change. It's often said that Shenzhen has no past, so can only look ahead. Rem Koolhaas, a Dutch architect who teaches at Harvard, called it the ultimate "generic city", a place without legacy that can swiftly adapt and grow with the times. But people I speak with, and academic reports, warn that the city's rapid transformation has turned it into a place with no identity, a place that is difficult to call home. On a daily basis, one can see how old buildings are being demolished to make way for modern structures.

When I visit Gothenburg, the town in Sweden where I was born, it mostly looks the same as it did when I was a boy. My old school and our old house are still there, even some neighbors. My son can play at the same playground and football pitch where my friends and I roamed around as kids. There are, naturally, tons of new restaurants, shops and residential areas, but the overall feeling of the city is the same. In Shenzhen, it's quite the opposite.

"There's nothing left of the area where I grow up. It's all gone", says a friend who is in her late 20s and was born in Shenzhen. "I have no places with childhood memories. I have no roots. And it makes me worried about the future."

It's not quite correct to say that Shenzhen has no history. Some areas of the city, so-called urban villages, have hundreds of years of history. One example is the ancient village of Hubei, which dates back some 500 years to the Ming Dynasty. But most of these urban villages – including neighbourhoods where some of the city's now-famed entrepreneurs started out – have already been demolished. Since Shenzhen is one of the country's hottest property markets, the land is gold for developers, government officials and anyone who can get a piece of the pie, legal or otherwise.

Home prices have more than doubled since 2014 – the fastest growth in residential property prices worldwide. Skyrocketing rents are identified as a major hindrance to the inflow of young talents to the city. Experts and municipal officials have also started to express concerns about businesses leaving the city. Without affordable accommodation, the founders of tomorrow's unicorns will have to go somewhere else.

During a conference in Hong Kong I talk with Ye Qing, one of the Shenzhen local government's top housing planning officials, about the future of affordable living for normal people. He says that the city plans to preserve several of the villages and raise living conditions there.

"Urban villages play a very important role in the development of Shenzhen. They provide the living environment that could cater to the needs of people from all walks of life", says Ye, who is director of the Shenzhen Institute of Building Research and the President of Shenzhen Green Building Association.

"We welcome companies from all over the world to participate in building green constructions in Shenzhen. Shenzhen is an open and inclusive city. Our city constructions aim to emulate international cities'. So we welcome companies which have advanced technologies in green construction."

Still, some 100 urban villages and 100 old industrial areas are currently earmarked for demolition by the local government. They will be revamped into modern, less affordable, neighborhoods. In 2016, the city built more skyscrapers than the entire United States.

"I love my city," my Shenzhen-born friend told me, "but sometimes everybody is just running too fast."

No wonder it's nick-named China's original "instant city".

ACKNOWLEDGEMENTS

This short e-book is mainly the result of many travels to Shenzhen and neighboring cities over several years, although most of the research and interviews are new. I have also used several sources to find relevant data, and I would give extra credit to The Economist's special report on the Silicon Delta, Flynn Murphy's in-depth article in Nature and news website TechNode, which covers tech in China better than anyone. I'd also like to give a massive shout out to all friends and good people in Shenzhen who opened doors for me in the city and showed great hospitality and friendliness.

Please sign up for launch of my next e-book: shenzhensuperstars.com

give credit to

DON'T FORGET MY FREE GIFT TO YOU

Just a friendly reminder. If you would like a unique list of co-working offices, accelerators, maker spaces and technology parks in Shenzhen, please e-mail me at shenzhensuperstars@gmail.com with subject FREE GIFT.

This is my way of saying thanks for purchasing this book.

Made in the USA
San Bernardino, CA
03 October 2018